California Crazy: Roadside Vernacular Architecture

JIM HEIMANN & RIP GEORGES
WITH AN INTRODUCTION BY DAVID GEBHARD

CALIFORNIA CRAZY

ROADSIDE VERNACULAR ARCHITECTURE

CHRONICLE BOOKS SAN FRANCISCO
PRINTED IN JAPAN

For Toots and Ollie—Roleen and Zoe
J.H.

For Ryan McPherson and Nancy Steiny
R.G.

CALIFORNIA CRAZY

Reprinted in 1985 by Dai Nippon, Tokyo
Copyright © 1980
Jim Heimann and Rip Georges.

Published by Chronicle Books.
One Hallidie Plaza
San Francisco, CA 94102

**Library of Congress Cataloging in
Publication Data**

Heimann, Jim, 1948–

    California Crazy
Bibliography: p. 131
Includes index.

1. Architecture, Modern–20th century–California. 2. Architecture–
California. 3. Vernacular architecture–California. 4. Restaurants, lunch
rooms, etc.–California. I. Georges, Rip,
1948-joint author. II. Title.

NA730. C2H4   725'71'09794
79-24181 ISBN 0-87701-171-0

ACKNOWLEDGMENTS

From inception to finish, the compilation of this book has been totally dependent on the cooperation and generosity of the people listed below. We would like to make special mention of the following people: David Gebhard for his total cooperation, suggestions, and enthusiasm throughout the project; Freda Wheatley Vizcarra for a perfect job of research, and for traipsing from Loma Linda to Pico Rivera to Turlock and back, all in the call of duty; Chris DeNoon for a rabid interest in researching in New York (and especially for finding the Wayside Salesman); Mary Ison of the Library of Congress, Alan Jutzi of the Huntington Library, Bonnie Rothbart of the M.G.M. Research Library, Victor Plukas of Security Pacific Bank, Dave Streeter of the Pomona Library, and Mark Wanamaker of the Bison Archives, for their help and for making their photo collections available to us; Delmar Watson, Bev Deminna, and Ed Whittington for sharing their incredible photo archives and anecdotes; to Arthur Whizin, owner and designer of the "Chili Bowls," for sharing his thoughts and personal memories. And finally to David Barich, Dick Schuettge, and Jane Vandenburgh for their faith and invaluable help throughout the project.

John Baeder

John Beach

Dick Bernet

David Boule

Genoa Caldwell
The Stock Market

John Cahoon
The Los Angeles County Museum of Natural History

John Chase

Art Curtis

Jim Deesing

Richard Gutman

Robert Hollingsworth
Burton Holmes Photography

Paul Ivory

Steven Izenour

Kenneth Kneitel

Gary Krueger

Chester Liebs

Richard Longstreth

John Margolis

Henry Marquez

Esther McCoy

Merriman Photography Co.

Alison Morley

The National Archives,
Washington D.C.

Tom Nikosey

Marvin Rand

John Reed

J.T. Steiny

Marc Treib

John Tullis

Henry Vizcarra

Laura Gest Winder

Robert Winter

CONTENTS

PAGE 11   INTRODUCTION

PAGE 26   CHAPTER I: PROGRAMATIC ARCHITECTURE

PAGE 82   CHAPTER II: PERIOD REVIVAL

PAGE 110   CHAPTER III: OUT-OF-STATE-ODDITIES

PAGE 121   AFTERWORD

PAGE 124   MAP OF EXISTING STRUCTURES

PAGE 127   NOTES

PAGE 131   BIBLIOGRAPHY

PAGE 137   INDEX

"If, when you went shopping, you found you could buy cakes in a windmill, ices in a gigantic cream-can, flowers in a huge flower-pot, you might begin to wonder whether you had not stepped through a looking glass or taken a toss down a rabbit burrow and could expect Mad Hatter or White Queen to appear round the next corner. But there would be nothing unreal about it if you were in Hollywood, South California, for shops of that kind are to be seen in all of the shopping districts there."[1] This reaction during the late 1930s by a Briton to Southern California is just one of the times when the Southland has been viewed as the land of exotica. From the 1870s on, that which has seemed startling and unique in Southern California has been cultivated by both natives and visitors so that myth has slowly become fact.

In the late nineteenth century the exotica of Southern California almost always cited were its tropical and semitropical vegetation which had been introduced to the land, and what seemed to be a looser, more carefree, mode of daily life. By the mid-1880s the exuberance (or, as some felt, madness) of architecture was added as another California oddity. In the early 1900s California as a place distinct from the rest of the U.S. became a major theme in its literature, arts and architecture. California's drippingly sentimental cultivation of the Mission Revival in architecture, followed by its passionate, indeed almost religious, conversion to the Spanish Colonial Revival in the 1920s were broad-scale efforts to make the contrast between the American East and Midwest as sharp and as startling as possible.

It could well be argued that the high point of California's stance as the land of the unique was directly tied to the emergence of California as Automobile-Land. In addition to providing the means of realizing suburbia, that greatest of American ideals, the automobile encouraged an entirely new response to how, on a day-to-day basis, we could experience our built or planted environment. California's mildness of climate, with the resulting ability to cheaply and quickly erect structures, encouraged a nonserious view of not only architecture, but symbolism and salesmanship as well. Why not make the process of selling and buying as lighthearted and enjoyable as other aspects of the free way of living which California had made possible?

And if Californians were going to be fully committed to this "auto-mania" (as it was called in the teens), then why not cultivate a set of architectural images which would instantly catch the eye, and which we would continue to remember? Driving by or attending a motion picture showing in Los Angeles at Grauman's Chinese Theater (Meyer and Holler, 1927) or at the Egyptian Theater (Meyer and Holler, 1922) or at the Mayan Theater (Morgan, Walls and Clements, 1928) was not an experience easily forgotten. Equally, a run by a tire manufacturing company posing as an Assyrian palace (Samson Tire

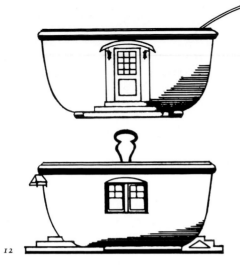

Chili Booth

Patent No. 83335
Volney A. McLaren
Wichita, Kansas, 1929

Building Design

Patent No. 94, 787
Andrew J. Stevens
Kansas City, Missouri, 1934

and Rubber Co., Morgan, Walls and Clements, 1929) was a far more effective way of pressing us to remember the product than a series of roadside billboards.

The introduction of the automobile made possible the linear, horizontal spread of Los Angeles with its resulting low density and low land values, and in the process it brought about the development of a wide range of auto-oriented, drive-in architecture. California, and Los Angeles in particular, did not originate auto-oriented signage and architecture, but its physical environment, its life-style, and its degree of commitment to the automobile made its ultimate fulfillment possible in the Southern California scene. As the New York-based editors of *The Architectural Forum* noted in an article, "Palaces of the Hot Doges," published in 1935, ". . .anything haywire is always most haywire in California."[2]

The quantity of written and spoken verbiage devoted to high art painting and sculpture published in our century has often led us to respond to their symbolic intent rather than their purely visual image. The truth is that the museum label, scholarly art historical slide presentation, or coffee-table monograph on a major artist often seems of greater importance than the object itself.

Except for a high art small elite, architecture has not yet experienced a similar wholesale transference of values from the world of form to the world of symbolism. So far the middle-class audience has not been pressed first to read an explanation of a building and then to go out and experience it. This is not to imply that direct and indirect symbolism does not exist in buildings, but rather that the visual language generally employed within our Western European architectural tradition has been a popular coinage generally understood by most members of society. In the twentieth century the architectural language of the Colonial Revival, English Tudor, French Norman, or Classical Beaux Arts has been, through its historical allusions, direct and understandable. Equally, buildings which were clothed in the garb of the new, ranging from the Art Nouveau, to the Zigzag (Art Deco) and Streamline Moderne, and the International Style (Modern) were addressed to a wide audience, ranging from the architectural elite to the middle class. In most instances these Period Revival or Modern buildings might well reveal layers of symbolic subtleties understood by only a few, but a knowledge of these subtleties was not necessary for a middle-class American to respond to the essential symbolism of each of these different images.

If we glance back into history and examine our European inheritance in architecture, we will find that the symbolic intent conveyed by buildings can (with just a little squeezing here and there) be placed in several separate pigeonholes. The largest of these compartments would accommodate the time-honored tradition of architectural borrowings or plagiarism from architecture's own past. The use of past architectural languages to comment on both the past and present is an overriding quality of the classical tradition of Greece and Rome itself. Equally, the

Refreshment Building

Patent No. 82865
Eugene L. Weaver
Los Angeles, California, 1930

direct and indirect borrowings experienced during the medieval period, and thence through the Renaissance to the present moment illustrate how the European tradition of architectural borrowing has been its dominant, most consistent theme.

A second, much smaller pigeonhole should be provided for symbolic borrowings which lie outside of the realm of traditional architectural language. These exterior borrowings range from zoological and botanical forms to those taken from the idealized realm of geometry such as spheres and squares. The entrance to a garden grotto through the mouth of a river monster, a multistory dwelling built as an elephant, or a sphere as a house, and, in our century, an enlarged hot dog as a fast-food restaurant are programatic devices meant to convey a set array of meanings. As with traditional architectural borrowings, the nonarchitectural images may well be resplendent with scholarly meaning, still they were meant to be readable by those who were to experience and use them.

Finally, there is another category of architectural borrowings that should be housed in its own tiny pigeonhole: these are those employing either elements of traditional architectural vocabulary or nontraditional forms to convey meaning by indirection. In the English Picturesque Garden Tradition of the eighteenth century, the miniature classical temple, the exotic Islamic kiosk, or the ruins of a medieval castle played a game of double transference. We were not being asked to respond to them in a straightforward fashion as examples of conventional architectural imagery; rather, their intent was to comment on the present and its relation to the past.

In the twentieth century a hotel built as an Aztec temple, or an enlarged ice cream cone used to sell ice cream employ similar elements of indirect symbolism. While the English Picturesque Garden was limited in its audience to the gentry who could read its meaning, such was not the case with most nontraditional architectural imagery in the twentieth century.

Before looking into the history of our nontraditional architectural borrowings it would be well to see if we could catalogue them in some fashion. The word "programatic" could be suggested as a possible all-embracing term to describe this specified approach to architectural language. The vocabulary employed in these buildings hinged on a program organized to convey meaning not directly but by indirection. The program of intent and the visual means employed were integral with one another. The audience then, was being asked to respond not to the artifact, but to the programatic utterance lying behind the form. In traditional architectural borrowings, by contrast, the means (style or fashion) employed had an existence in its own right, regardless of other accumulated meanings which might be ascribed to it.

Programatic borrowings of the past divided themselves into two basic sources —those emanating from the world of high art and those derived from low art. Within our European tradition the principal low art examples have been signs to advertise and sell services and merchandise. For the literate as well as an illiterate audience a hanging sign

13

Barbeque Stand

Patent No. 90303
William H. Alston
San Antonio, Texas, 1933

in the form of a boot was a far more effective way of letting us know that this is a shoe shop than using the written word. A sign in the symbolic form of the product was a well-used device not only in the Middle Ages, but also in ancient Rome, and it has continued as a common mode of communication right down to the present.

Alongside this programatic, one-to-one symbolism has been another convention of employing signs which expressed the name of the establishment. An inn whose name was "The Head of the Horse," might well advertise its presence by a cutout, slightly sculptured sign in the form of a horse's head. In the nineteenth century the scale of these programatic signs was dramatically increased. Large sculptured forms might surmount or be placed in front of a building, directly or indirectly indicating its usage. As a case in point, in the 1890s the Eleventh Street Branch of the Grand Central Market, in Oakland, California, boasted a fully sculptured, brightly painted cow which was three times the size of a real cow.[3]

A second source from our European past came out of the high art world of architecture and landscape architecture. The villa gardens of Imperial Rome confronted their visitors with fountains and grottos often in the form of real and mythical animals, humans and plants. Topiary—the sculpting of vegetation into forms of animals and other exotica—was another time-honored tradition. Pliny the Younger, writing of his own villa garden at Tusulan speaks of trees ". . .cut into a variety of names and shapes."[4] The Roman tradition of topiary continued on through the Middle Ages, and it was utilized with renewed enthusiasm during the Renaissance. In the sixteenth century and later, the specific symbolic Roman usage of garden structures in the form of fantastic humans and animals came once more into play. It crept into the urban environment where in the 1593 Palazzo Zuccari in Rome, visitors entered the Palazzo through the mouth of an anxiously awaiting monster.

High art's principal contribution to Programatic architecture occurred in the eighteenth century in the English Picturesque Garden tradition and in the work at the end of that century of the classical Visionary architects.[5] These architects pursued three versions of Programatic architecture. Their dominant commitment was to the world of geometry transformed—transformed in scale, and put to factual and symbolic usages. Claude-Nicolas Ledoux's often illustrated quarters for the rural caretakers of the 1780s, in the form of a free-standing sphere, disassociated from the landscape, is an example which immediately comes to mind. The single geometric form of the sphere, symbolic of geometry, could also be enshrouded with an overlay of other meanings. Etienne-Louis Booleé's Memorial to Isaac Newton (1784) used the sphere to symbolize the Newtonian view of the universe, while Ledoux employed the sphere in his Plan for a Cemetery (1773-79) to evoke a sense of death and the underworld. These French, German, English and American visionary architects employed a full package of programatic tricks to yank and pull us out of the world of everyday reality. Traditional architectural elements and parts

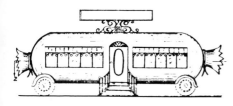

Tamale Inn

Patent No. 78424
Samuel C. Wilhite
Los Angeles, California, 1928

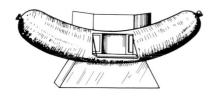

Vending Stand

Patent No. 78662
Anthony Soucie
Oakland, California, 1928

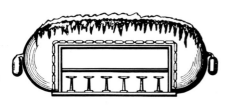

Restaurant

Patent No. 87080
Rex La Payne
Glendale, California, 1932

of buildings were raised to a scale diverging from reality. Forms were borrowed from man's real or mythical past or from the faraway worlds of China, India and the Near East. Buildings which borrowed from entirely non-traditional architectural imagery included Ledoux's Woodcutter's House and Workshop (1773-79) in the form of a pyramidal stack of wood, Bouleé's Cenotaph for a Warrior (undated), where we are confronted with a classical sarcophagus which has been blown up into a large building, and finally Jean-Jacques Lequeu's Barn in the Form of a Cow (undated).

The nineteenth century continued this high art tradition of Programatic architecture in only a marginal way. Certain pure geometric forms, such as the octagon, enjoyed great popularity, but the programatic exoticism of this form became so watered down in fact and symbolic content, that most people of the time responded to it within its own advertised realm of supposed rationalism and utility. By the 1880s the exoticism of the non-European architectural languages—Islamic, Chinese and Japanese—had become so commonplace in the way they were used that they could only marginally be thought of as Programatic.

In contrast, the popular nineteenth-century scene provided a much stronger continuity between the distant past and our century. Signage—in scale, lavishness, and in sheer quantity—put the pre-1800 world to shame. Nowhere was this more true than in the United States where by the end of the century immense thirty- to forty-foot billboards were erected in towns and cities. Antici-pating the billboards was the convention of painting signs directly on the walls of buildings; it was in the latter half of the nineteenth century that this practice was expanded so that entire walls of commercial buildings and rural barns were transformed into giant advertising signs.

An important link in the upward and inward progress of Programatic buildings was a few structures in the form of elephants and other creatures, the most widely known being James F. Lafferty's come-on elephant "Lucy" built at South Atlantic City (Margate City) in 1881.[6] Lafferty's sixty-five-foot creation was modeled on the designs of the French architect Charles-Francois Ribart for a garden kiosk in the form of an elephant which were published in 1758. Ribart's creature served as a symbol of the triumphs of the French crown; Lafferty's nineteenth-century elephant sold real estate.

Around the turn of the century there was an increase of Programatic buildings in the amusement promenades of national and international expositions and in a growing number of amusement parks. The impact of these buildings tended to be somewhat different, for they existed in a noneveryday environment: their visual amusement or shock was minimal compared to what happens when these unfamiliar forms pop up in our everyday world.

During the twentieth century it was the introduction of the automobile which promoted a new wave of direct Programatic architecture. Not only did the coming of the automobile encourage the Programatic, it could even participate in its spirit as in 1911 when the

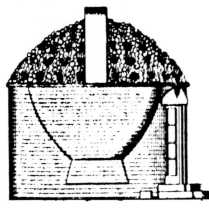

Building

Patent No. 77141
Warren E. Wolfe
Los Angeles, California, 1928

California Corrugated Culvert Company of San Francisco had its company car built in the form of a corrugated culvert, which by chance happened to have an engine and four wheels.[7] The usage of enlarged sculptured products to sell, which had begun in the nineteenth century, was raised both physically and symbolically to new heights in the first two decades of this century. In Indianapolis, a milk company constructed two fifty-two-foot-high milk bottles of glazed bricks, and other smaller-scale milk bottles, beer jugs and wine bottles began to appear along America's developing systems of highways.[8] It was during the next two decades, the 1920s and 1930s, that the many forms of Programatic architecture were firmly ensconced on the scene. Though there were examples built on the Continent and in England, it was the U.S., and especially the West Coast, which brought forth most of the examples.

The popular version of the modern, the Zigzag Moderne (Art Deco) of the twenties and of the early thirties introduced Programatic elements into its buildings. In that gem of the Moderne—the Chrysler building in New York (1930)—the architect William Van Alen established a Programatic decorative program of ". . .glorifying American mechanical genius and incidentally Mr. Chrysler's output of cars, trucks and boats."[9] Radiator caps and emblems were used for flagpole sockets and ". . .on the thirteenth story, the brickwork wheels revolved under horizontal mud guards. . . ."[10] In Los Angeles, the Sunset Towers, one of the city's major contributions to the Moderne (Leland

A. Bryant, 1929-31), helps us to locate the enclosed parking garage by placing terracotta automobile fronts below and above the windows.

The exponents of the Moderne maneuvered themselves even closer to the pretenses of high art in their frequent uses of programatic sculpture. Sculpture depicting specific historic individuals from classical and nonclassical sources was a favored device of the European and American Beaux Arts tradition from the 1890s through the 1930s. But such figures demand some degree of humanistic erudition so that the audience could fully comprehend what was supposedly symbolized. The elaborate sculptural program worked out for the Nebraska State Capital Building in Lincoln by Bertram G. Goodhue, the philosopher Hartley Burr Alexander and the sculptor Lee Lawrie added the remote highfalutin reference to the past expected of a public building, but, because of its limited audience, this approach certainly could not be used to sell an everyday product of American industry.[11] As a rule, the popular architectural sculpture of American Moderne generally assumed a more programatic approach. The four tympanum figures over the entrance to Los Angeles' black and gold Richfield building (Morgan, Walls and Clements, 1928) symbolized Aviation, Postal Service, Industry, and Navigation—all of course powered by oil.[12] These classically inspired figures were made understandable (it was hoped) by adding wings and a propeller to the figure of Aviation, and by attaching similar easily recognizable appendages to the other three figures.

California Crazy

Refreshment Stand

Patent No. 93665
Warren Lee
Los Angeles, California, 1934

Building

Patent No. 85006
Chester A. Sanborn
Lynn, Massachusetts, 1930

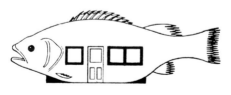

Vending Structure

Patent No. 95314
Alfred H. Burks
Dayton, Ohio

The play between the innuendos of high art and direct programatic art was a theme which occurred with moderate frequency in roadside advertising of the 1920s. The serious-minded lamented what they saw happening to the roadside. With the completion of an extensive portion of a national highway system by the early 1930s the advantages of regional and national repetitive highway signage came into the picture. The most extravagant of these were the sequential Burma Shave signs with their quizzical utterances luring the driver to the final Burma Shave sign, and sign notices throughout the upper Midwest ending one up in Wall's Drug Store in Wall, South Dakota. The imagery of the Burma Shave signage was fitting for a national product while the Wall's Drug Store signs had an appropriate fallen-down Western look.

The California architect Robert H. Orr noted that the way things were going, ". . .our highways, byways and street corners will be lined with sculptural monuments revealing those strewn along the 'Holy Way' to the ancient Tombs of the Mings."[13] What Orr was referring to were three-dimensional sculptural advertising signs usually consisting of a high base which bore the written message, and sculptural horses and riders, bulls, or racing cars placed on top. In some instances there was an understandable relationship between the sculpture above and whatever it advertised, as the figure of a bull helped name Ye Bull Penn Inn in Los Angeles, or a depiction of Barney Oldfield and his racing car to help sell Richfield gasoline. In other instances, "famous" statuary was taken from the world of

high art with seemingly no direct connection (other than the prestige of "Art") between the sculpted figure and the advertising product. The inventiveness of Programatic signage was especially evident in the 1930s. In 1931 the Coca Cola Company used real-life female models to sit under make-believe palm trees to enjoy the "pause that refreshed."[14] The play between that which is and that which is not was frequently employed in large billboard signage where real objects occurred within an illusionary painted sign. The General Sign Company of Oakland placed a coupe from the Howard Motor Company within a tropical island setting complete with a sunset, and on the roadside outside of Milwaukee, there was a real yellow and silver airplane, apparently crashing into the ground. This eye-catcher let the passing motorist know it was only a twenty minute drive to Schuster's Department Store.[15] A subtle, complex interchange between the real and illusionary occurred in a large sign in Indianapolis, where a gigantic make-believe mirror enlarged a moving sequence of views of the individual shops located in the Circle Tower Shopping Center. In this instance the signage with its movement accentuated by changing colored lights existed as an intermediator between the potential customer and the actual passage into the individual shops.[16]

Another twentieth century link with the Programatic architecture of the past is to be found in the use of architectural imagery which was either exotic (the faraway or far-distant past), or was a perversion of some past European architectural mode. Forms which we

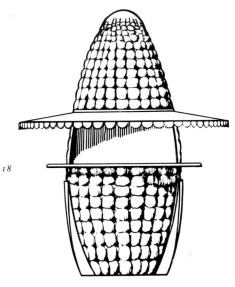

Booth

Patent No. 100333
John M. Miller
Bend, Oregon, 1936

would loosely label as "medieval" were a favorite imagery of the 1920s. But this medieval imagery was meant to be read through our remembrances of the fairy-tale world of Hansel and Gretel.[17] These little witches' cottages—which might serve as real estate offices, service stations, or fast-food restaurants—play an intriguing game with scale and other make-believe elements. They are, in fact, dollhouses enlarged, but kept at distances from the world of traditional imagery.

The range of non-European traditional imagery utilized during the twenties reveals that through popular magazines (especially *The National Geographic* for the American middle-class audience) the world architectural scene was just waiting to be grabbed up. The rash of eighteenth-and nineteenth-century non-European borrowings was continued, although the context was meant to be more jarring, so that their indirect message could be more favorably conveyed. Egypt, Babylonia, Assyria, Japan, China, and Hindu and Islamic India provided vocabularies for anything ranging from the interior of restaurants to motion picture theaters. Added to these older borrowings was a new group of "primitive" images derived from the Pacific world of Melanesia and Polynesia, the pre-European pueblos of the American Southwest, the tepees of the Plains Indians, and the Pre-Columbian architecture of the Maya, the Zapotec and the Aztec of Mexico and Central America.

During the thirties these exotic borrowings were joined and almost overwhelmed by the imagery of the Streamline Moderne. The Streamline Moderne, as a popular architectural system of imagery, seized upon the element of speed—epitomized in the aerodynamic design of the airplane—and applied it to the full range of designed products, including signage and large and small buildings. Even signs were caught up in the Streamlining urge: ". . .if outdoor advertising is to keep its foremost place among advertising mediums it must keep its foremost place in design, too, along with motor cars and airplanes and railroad trains."[18] That which distinguishes the Streamline Moderne has to do with how the audience was asked to respond to the building. In the case of a Streamline Moderne building the audience was expected to see it as architecture which had been clothed in a modern garb. Programatic Streamline Moderne buildings exist in the form, for example, of a streamlined train as a diner, a streamlined boat as a restaurant, or a streamlined automobile as a service station.[19] By the end of the 1930s the Streamline Moderne image, with its hint at what glories lay in store for us in the future, had almost entirely supplanted the older languages of Programatic architecture.

An illustration of how the twenties could be tied to the thirties and how the past could be linked to the future can be seen in the many fast-food hamburger shops in the form of streamlined castles. The single corner tower used for the chain of White Tower Hamburger Shops was all that was needed to suggest that it was medieval.[20] The Wichita-based White Castle buildings played off the hygienic quality of white porcelain panels against crenelated parapet and tower, while the Tulsa-based Silver

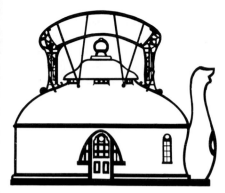

Tea House

Patent No. 81862
Ernest F. Schreiber
Omaha, Nebraska, 1930

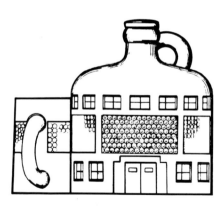

Refreshment Building

Patent No. 108550
Terrence R. Morgan
Vancouver, Washington, 1937

Castle chain ended up with a totally streamlined box which retained its allegiance to the medieval past solely through its name and logo.[21]

Turning our attention specifically to California's Programatic architecture of the twenties and thirties, it is of interest to note that these Programatic forms came onto the scene late in the 1920s, and more of them were built during the opening years of the Great Depression than before. Though there were examples before 1928, their high point was between 1928 and 1934. This is borne out not only by examples which were constructed but by the numerous unbuilt examples for which patents were issued.[22] The ingenuity of American designers is pointedly and delightfully revealed in the array of "impossible" visual images which they patented. What was built in California and elsewhere in the country reveals only the tip of the iceberg in terms of America's faith in the Programatic to sell services and products. Lunchpails, jugs, teapots and cups, locks and keys, corncobs, milk bottles, ice cream cones and freezers, birthday cakes, icebergs, soup bowls, oranges, hot dogs, and tamales were joined by dogs, pigs and dancing girls as constructions. There also were the machine themes applied to buildings: airplanes, ships, automobiles, and even spark plugs and light bulbs.

If we apply our earlier categories to these examples, buildings and signs generally fall into two basic groups—those whose imagery directly conveys what was being sold, and those which employed a wide variety of indirect messages to advertise. All of the Programatic structures, whether a tamale stand built in the form of a tamale, or an airplane built as a service station, were created to be eye-catchers: they were meant to startle, shock and amuse. Humor was an essential element in the audience's response to these structures. Even the streamlined passenger car as a diner, with its allusions to the future, was meant to convey a sort of lighthearted Buck Rogers excursion.

Direct Programatic architecture—the structure as a sign of what it was selling —succeeded because of the simplicity of its symbolism, whereas indirect Programatic architecture entailed degrees of meaning which, one suspects, had the potential of holding the audience's attention for a longer period of time. An enlarged dog which sold hot dogs exemplifies a first step in the process of injecting indirect meaning into the architectural vocabulary. An iceberg to sell cold soft drinks and ice cream or a teapot or coffeepot built as a restaurant suggests that this is a place where food and drink may be obtained. A service station in the shape of an airplane asks that the audience symbolically connect two machines with the selling and consuming of energy-producing products.

All of these buildings somehow manage to maintain connections between the form of the structure and what is being advertised, but such is not the case for a wide variety of exotic languages which often occurs in Programatic architecture. An owl enlarged to a small building, which housed an ice cream stand reveals no connection between product and the form of the building. Perhaps, it might be suggested, there is a linkage to be found in

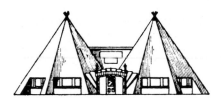

Resort Building

Patent No. *105823*
Herman E. Olson
Seattle, Washington, 1937

Booth

Patent No. *83838*
Ralph R. Van Dusen
Wichita, Kansas, 1930

the childhood world of fairy tales, reinforced in the twenties and thirties by the dream world of the Hollywood motion picture. The architectural garb provided in Los Angeles by Grauman's Chinese Theatre, the Egyptian Theatre, and that of the Mayan Theatre, was openly employed to carry the theatre-goer into an intermediary noneveryday world, and thence into the visual mythology of the film. The far-distant lands of the Egyptians, of the Mayans and the Chinese were, by the mid-twenties, a more effective device to carry the audience into the film than the earlier usage of the sumptuous Beaux Arts baroque.

The most prevalent building types associated with Programatic architecture were those associated with the automobile and drive-in architecture. Here the need for quick identification at a reasonable speed and distance meant that a building which would catch the eye, could or should draw in the customers. In writing about Pasadena's well-known Mother Goose Pantry (1929) which was built as a great shoe, a writer noted that ". . .[Foothill] Boulevard is lined with wayside places of various types and designs for miles. Everyone of these is forgotten, however, save the famous Mother Goose Pantry . . . .No human being with a fraction of imagination could forget the Mother Goose Pantry."[23]

A theme which enjoyed great popularity throughout the U.S. was that of the frontier log cabin. One of the earliest of these in California was the 1911 Old Log Cabin refreshment stand in San Diego. Numerous variations on this theme were carried out in California in the 1920s and 1930s, including buildings in the form of a single tree trunk. In 1930 the log cabin was seized upon as an architectural style for a chain of small fast-food restaurants, the White Log Taverns. The first of these was built in Oakland and, by 1937, there were sixty-two of these fast-food restaurants located throughout California.[24] The White Log Taverns, with their frames of steel sheathed in concrete logs, played off two sets of images—that of the log cabin and that of the American Colonial Style. For a national image, this added up to the best of two worlds. Another California example of the virtues of the American home and the frontier was The Big Fireplace drive-in restaurant in Los Angeles (1927), which greeted its customers with two giant-scale exterior fireplaces augmented by a pattern of everchanging red lights. The parking lot and street had become one great American living room.[25]

More indicative of the California scene, and especially of Southern California, was the occurrence of Hansel and Gretel architecture. The first of these buildings on the Los Angeles scene was designed by Henry Oliver who was a set designer for Metro-Goldwyn-Meyer Studios. In 1921 he designed the studio offices for Irwin C. Willit Productions in Culver City. "We have tried," noted Irvin C. Willit, "to reproduce a tumble-down structure of two centuries ago, but which will be equipped with the most modern office appurtenances."[26] The reason for this cultivated architectural exoticism was no different than that for a drive-in restaurant. A 1921 newspaper article of the time reported, "It is said that this structure has occasioned more com-

Building

Patent No. 86683
Sadie O'Neil
Seattle, Washington, 1931

ments from passing motorists than any building erected in Los Angeles in recent months."[27]

Within the next year Oliver went on to design the first of the Van de Kamp's Bakery's famous shingle-covered windmills, and the Tam O'Shanter Restaurant located on Los Feliz near Griffith Park.[28] The Tam O'Shanter Restaurant was supposedly California's first drive-in restaurant, and it was the first of the Los Angeles drive-ins to consciously cultivate the world of Alice in Wonderland.[29] Its fairy-tale atmosphere was openly connected at the time to Hollywood: "...The Tam O'Shanter Restaurant is a product of movie town architecture efficiently applied."[30]

In the late twenties and early thirties movieland versions of Hansel and Gretel cottages were built throughout the West Los Angeles area, many of which were designed by the productive and professionally respected firm of Pierpont and Walter S. Davis. Robert H. Derrah, who is best remembered for his Coca Cola Company building in the form of a streamlined ocean liner, employed the Alice in Wonderland theme for his Continental Villa, which formed a segment of his 1936 Cross Roads of the World on Sunset.[31] Half-timbered medievalism continued on into the post-World War II years, but these later examples establish their relationship to the traditional world of architectural imagery, rather than to the storybook world of Alice or Hansel and Gretel.

In the East, South and Midwest, the colonial was by far the favored image for a wide variety of small roadside commercial buildings, ranging from service stations to restaurants. In Cali-

fornia the imagery of the colonial was occasionally used as in Fatty Arbuckles' Plantation Cafe of 1926 on Washington Boulevard. In this case, it was the signage on the roof and the signing on the long low mound of turf which pull the structure and its setting out of the normal world of architecture. That this perversion of the past has not left us is readily apparent in the 1960 Pacific Savings (now California Federal Savings) designed by Rick Farver Associates where the fullblown vestige of George Washington's Mt. Vernon has been moved from the shores of the Potomac to a safe site overlooking the Hollywood Freeway.

Most instances of California's Mission, Hispanic and Mediterranean imagery used for small scale commercial purposes tended to be rather straight forward interpretations of one or another of these modes. Just off the path of traditional architecture were those marginal establishments which employed the Pueblo Revival, the Moorish or Islamic Revival and the Pre-Columbian of Mexico and Central America. Gay's Lion Farm (1926) in El Monte, and, above all, the impossible Cliff Dwellers Cafe on Beverly Boulevard (1927) illustrate how a non-European architectural image could be pulled into the realm of the Programatic. Equally strained in its relationship to the traditional were a wide array of Islamic-inspired designs: the Calmos #1 Service Station (1925) on Hollywood Boulevard with its domed mosque-like station which is accompanied by two minarets; and Roland E. Coate's Calpet Service Station (1928) on Wilshire Boulevard where the final touch was the female

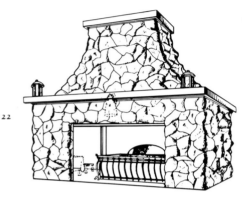

Store

Patent No. 80063
Harry E. Webb
Buffalo, New York, 1928

Moorish attendants who serviced your Packard or Franklin. The Islamic theme was employed for King's Tropical Inn on Washington Boulevard (1926), which somehow sought to connect its specialty of chicken dinners with the exotic world of Africa and the Near East. In the thirties, the imagery of the land of the Arabian Nights encouraged an Iranian mosque for the Beverly Theatre (1930-31) and for the extensive offices of the Girard Real Estate Development (1928) on Ventura Boulevard.

While the downtown Mayan Theatre was locally the most widely known of Los Angeles' Pre-Columbian exercises, the most extensively written about was Robert Stacy-Judd's Aztec Hotel (1926) in Monrovia.[32] The delightful and at times humorously mad maneuvering of historic images can be seen if we compare the Oriental theme of the Mandarin Market (1929-30) on Vine and Grauman's Chinese Theatre, or the Egyptian assertions of Glendale's Egyptian Village Cafe (1924), and the Egyptian Theatre in Hollywood. A recurring theme in eighteenth-century architecture was the return to the primitive, symbolized by the wood and thatched hut. Primitive or indigenous architecture was also played upon as a theme in Programatic architecture of the twenties and later. These images ranged from colorful Arab tents used to sell tropical fruits and juices, to thatched restaurants offering South Seas cuisine. The theme with the widest popular appeal was the Plains Indian tepee. Here was a form which was natively American and was closely tied to the romance of the West. To spend the night in a tepee motel or have one's car serviced at a tepee village

was a marvelous way to imply a connection between the nomadic Plains Indians, the westward movement of covered wagons and the automobile and the open highway.

Los Angeles' gift to America of buildings and signage represents a mixed-up world of myth and fact. Promotional trade, popular and professional publications obviously delighted in illustrating Los Angeles roadside buildings in the form of oranges, jugs and flower pots. Photographs of these Programatic buildings not only presented startling visual objects to their readers, but there was always the implication that the buildings illustrated were typical of the scene.[33] As artifacts of the roadside scene these Programatic buildings often lack the usual documentation associated with larger, more conventional, buildings. It is unlikely that we will ever know just how many of them were actually built. Altogether there were probably less than seventy-five Programatic buildings built in Southern California. What strikes one in looking through the published illustrations of these buildings is that only a small handful—less than a dozen—were illustrated over and over again. Generally the buildings which were repeatedly published were the most flamboyant, though one often has a sneaking suspicion that these were the Programatic buildings which by chance happened to have been photographed. While the Hoot Hoot Ice Scream stand in the form of an owl was located on Long Beach Boulevard, this was not a street which would normally be traveled by casual visitors to Los Angeles. Thus the picture presented at the time and later

Booth

Patent No. *107561*
Daniel G. Terrie
Rockville Centre, New York

Building

Patent No. *81403*
Rufus B. Rawlings
El Paso, Texas, 1929

that Los Angeles and Southern California highways and streets were lined by hundreds of Programatic buildings was simply not true.

The chronological history of Programatic buildings in California closely follows the pattern already mentioned in the discussion of traditional architectural imagery. One of the earliest examples was Albert Kenney's 1903-04 restaurant ship "Cabrillo" and Venetian Garden which was situated on the Venice pier.[34] This make-believe ship on piles pretended at one moment to be a Spanish galleon, at the next it was a fragment of a Venetian palace. By 1920 Kenney's ship "Cabrillo" was joined by a small scattering of buildings and three-dimensional signs situated in both Northern and Southern California. An often repeated theme was the building in the form of a milk bottle, but other exotica—oranges, artichokes and pumpkins—entered the scene.

The heyday of California's Programatic buildings occurred during the ten-year period from 1925 through 1934. It was in these years that the most famous of the California examples were built: the Hoot Hoot Ice Scream building (1925); the Brown Derby restaurant (1926); the Sphinx Realty building (1927); the Igloo building (1928); the Tamale building (1928); the Mother Goose Pantry restaurant (1929); the Zep Diner building (1930); the Toed Inn stand (1931); and the Pig Cafe (1934). While there were a few buildings constructed after 1935—such as Cobb's Chicken House at the 1939 San Francisco World Fair—which directly continued this earlier tradition, later Programatic transformations looked al-

most exclusively to the Streamlined Moderne image of the transportation machine for sources. In Los Angeles, Robert H. Derrah's streamlined ocean-liner for the Coca Cola Building (1936), was the grandest example, while all that was needed was a set of tracks for the streamlined train engine of Alice Faye's Club Car Restaurant (1941) to streak off into the night.[35] The image of the airplane, as the most advanced transportation machine, was employed for service stations, and in 1939 Charlie Le Maire, the Los Angeles restauranteur, patented the Skyline Diner, which was in the form of a Norman Bel Geddes' double-decked streamlined airplane.[36] The Dark Room (1938) on Wilshire moves us programatically into the objects sold by employing a streamlined image of a camera as its storefront.

When building activities resumed in California in 1945 after the war, there was almost a complete absence of Programatic buildings. The often illustrated Tail of the Pup on La Cienega Boulevard was built or refurbished in 1946, the Wigwam Village in Rialto was built in 1955, along with a few others—just enough examples to indicate that, although low keyed, the tradition was not dead.[37] The image of the doughnut as a symbol for fast food entered the California scene in 1954 with The Big Do-Nut chain, and numerous variations were built like The Do-Nut Hole (1958) in the City of Industry. In more recent years the older Programatic buildings have been joined by the Shutterbug (1977) in Westminster, and by the giant Caterpillar as a tractor salesroom in Turlock (1978).[38] There was, though, no break in California's usage

Igloo

Patent No. 81860
John Henry Whitington
Los Angeles, California, 1928

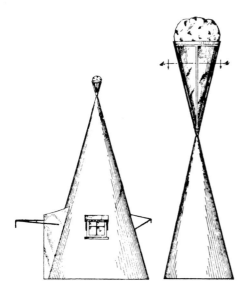

Ice Cream Stand

Patent No. 73563
Lawrence A. Fleming
Fairmont, West Virginia, 1927

of Programatic signage between the pre- and post-World War II years. The early Programatic signage of a wide-eyed puppy dog which looks down at us from atop Barkies Sandwich Shops (1930-31), was augmented in the Post-War period by the giant woman's leg which lets us know that this is indeed Sanderson's Stockings (1948), and by the red and white Santa Claus (1954) which announces that this is the town of Santa Claus, California.

Variations on this form of architecture signage were large-scale billboards and entire building facades which formed sculptured signs. Clifton's Cafeteria on Olive Street in downtown Los Angeles (1931) with its waterfalls, geysers and tropical foliage was matched, if not surpassed by the scene of romping and frolicking pigs which in painted and sculpted forms crawl over the walls and buildings of Farmer John's Meat Packing Plant in Vernon.[39]

The approach taken to language in these Programatic buildings or in signage ran the gamut between direct commentary to the exotic. The building in the form of the product sold—a tamale, orange or lemon is as obvious as one could ask. The next step of symbolism plays on the theme of the container or mechanism used in the production of the product: the flowerpot as a nursery or flower store, a cream can to sell dairy products; or a hand-cranked freezer to dispense ice cream products. A third set of symbols goes one step further by hinting at some quality associated with the product: an igloo and iceberg to sell cold drinks and ice cream, or a coffeepot to advise the viewer that this is a restaurant.

Then there are those buildings that comment on their names—The Brown Derby, The Toed Inn, or The Pig Cafe. There is often an essential need for the Programatic form of the building to be accompanied in this case by written signage so that the potential customer can tie the form and name together. Behind this play between the form and the written word is another element of attraction as to the whys and wherefores of the name itself. The shoe as a building for Pasadena's Mother Goose Pantry Restaurant is meant to pull us directly back into childhood.

But what levels of humorous meanings lie behind such themes as the Round House Cafe (1927), with its train engine plunging out toward us, or the World War I theme of a crashed airplane and sandbagged trenches of The Dugout (1927) in Montebello? The child's world of the fairy tale certainly lies behind The Mushrooms Restaurant (1928) in Burbank, and the Pumpkin Palace restaurant (1927) in Burbank, but other themes like the walled and guarded Jail Cafe (1926) must somehow appeal to other parts of our sensibilities. The suggestion that there should be a give-and-take between the real, everyday world and some other world was the overriding theme of California's Programatic excursion into the Streamline transportation machine. In the instances of streamlined ships, trains and airplanes of the late thirties and early forties we are asked to hop, skip and jump back and forth between the then-existing world of technology, the world of Buck Rogers and Flash Gordon, and the machine-dominated futurism of the twenty-first century.

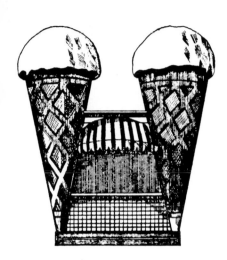

Ice Cream Stand

Patent No. 75511
George H. Natzel
Santa Anna, California, 1928

Programatic architecture and signage were almost universally condemned by America's upper middle class, professional planners, and the high art world. The first two groups felt (and quite rightly so) that Programatic structures, like billboards and roadside architecture in general, would destroy the City Beautiful sense of order in an urban environment, as well as the sylvan quality of suburbia. They were uncomfortable with the blatant commercialism these structures implied. The proponents of high art were afraid that the frequent use of sculpture in this fashion would debase the original, asking "Will they not eventually make sculpture. . . so commonplace that the real object of art, cannot, except by those especially trained, be disassociated from the commonplace and cause a decadency far-reaching in its effect and influence?"[40] In a way of course, this is just what happened. Bit by bit the high art world of Cubism, Futurism, and, above all, Dadaism, Surrealism and Pop has so mixed, transformed, and been transformed, that today a high arter and a good bourgeois will respond with equal ardor to those few remaining vestiges of our Programatic near-past.

It was the foremost of America's architectural historians, Henry Russell Hitchcock who as early as 1936 noted that, "The combination of strict functionalism and bold symbolism in the best roadside stands provides, perhaps, the most encouraging sign for the architecture of the Mid-twentieth century."[41] This affirmative response went basically unheeded and did not reappear until the 1950s in the pages of *Landscape* which was founded and edited by J.

Brickerhoff Jackson. Jackson, and the writers he assembled in the pages of *Landscape*, asked us to reassess the whole of our commercial vernacular including the highway and the commercial strip.[42] The imperative which Hitchcock had in mind for Programatic architecture finally arrived in the mid-sixties through the publication of Robert Venturi's volume, *Complexity and Contradiction in Architecture*, and in the buildings which he and his associates design.[43] Venturi's Duck (Martin H. Maurer's Roadside Stand near Riverhead, Long Island, 1933), symbolizing buildings as signs, brought the whole of Programatic buildings back into high-art respectability.[44] Since the early seventies the Programatic tradition of borrowing from architectural imagery itself and from outside of it has returned with a fervor. In California it seems almost to be a repeat of what occurred in the relationship of the use of programatic forms within the eighteenth-century English Picturesque Garden tradition, and the later occurrence of "real" Programatic buildings. In the 1950s California began to experience a rash of miniature golf courses resplendent with a wonderful array of toy-sized buildings; by the mid-seventies they began to be supplemented by "real" buildings. Whether the rich treasure trove of California's Programatic buildings will provide a similar inspiration for the present remains to be seen. One hopes it will.

David Gebhard
Director, University of
California Art Museum
Santa Barbara, California

CHAPTER ONE: PROGRAMATIC ARCHITECTURE

THE SOMBRERO

Location: Tijuana, Mexico
Circa 1928

California Crazy

LITTLE MARY'S LIGHTHOUSE REALTY

Location: 6002 Hollywood Boulevard, Hollywood
Circa 1922

SANDER'S SYSTEM BEN HUR COFFEE POT

Owner: Harry Carpenter
Location: 8531 Wilshire Boulevard, Beverly Hills
Date: 1930

California Crazy

THE HOT CHA

Location: 957 Fourth Street, Long Beach
Date: 1936

THEODORE SCHOOL OF MUSIC

Owner: Theodore Pezzolo
Location: 1666 Union Street, San Francisco
Date: 1958

California Crazy

MANNING'S BIG RED PIANO

Owner: "Doc" Manning
Architect: Frank H. Gaw
Location: Venice Boulevard at Oxford Street, Los Angeles
Date: 1930

THE CHILI BOWL

Owner: Arthur Whizin
Designer: Arthur Whizin
Contractor: Joe Lamb
Location: 3012 Crenshaw Boulevard, Los Angeles
Opened April 4, 1931

THE TAMALE

Location: 6421 Whittier Boulevard, Montebello
Date: 1928

TAIL O' THE PUP

Location: 311 North LaCienega, West Hollywood
Date: 1946

California Crazy

THE BROWN DERBY

Owner: Herbert Somborn
Location: 3427 Wilshire Boulevard, Los Angeles
Date: 1926

THE AIRPLANE CAFE

Location: U.S. 101, Los Angeles
Circa 1927

ZEP DINER

Location: 515 West Florence Avenue, Los Angeles
Date: 1930

DESCHWANDEN'S SHOE REPAIR

Location: Chester and 10th Streets, Bakersfield
Date: 1947

SANDERSON'S HOSIERY

Location: 11711 Olympic Boulevard
Date: February 1948

California Crazy

THE RED KEG DRIVE-IN

Location: 10635 West Washington Boulevard, Culver City
Date: 1935

THE KNOCKOUT

Owner: Warner Brothers Productions
Location: Motion picture set
Date: 1979

44

California Crazy

OIL PATCH LIQUOR

Owners: Bill and Diane Westby
Location: 2799 East Willow, Signal Hill
Date: 1976

THE IGLOO

Location: 4302 West Pico Boulevard, Los Angeles
Date: 1928

THE ICE PALACE

Location: 3400 Crenshaw Boulevard, Los Angeles
Circa 1929

California Crazy

THE DARKROOM

Location: 5730 Wilshire Boulevard, Los Angeles
Date: 1938

THE SHUTTER SHACK

Owner: Susan Del Monte
Designer: Susan Del Monte
Location: 15336 Golden West Street, Westminster
Date: 1977

TOED INN

Location: 12008 Channel Road, Santa Monica Canyon
Date: 1931

THE DOG CAFE

Location: 1153 West Washington Boulevard, Los Angeles
Circa 1928

California Crazy

RANDY'S DONUT

Owner: Lowey Baking Company
Original Location: 805 West Manchester, Inglewood
Date: 1954

THE DONUT HOLE

Location: 15300 East Amar Road, La Puente

NOAH'S ARK

Location: Highway 76 (East of Oceanside, California)
Circa 1945

MOUNT BALDY INN

Owners: Gar McOmber and W.A. Schenck
Location: 9608 Whittier Boulevard, Pico Rivera
Date: April 9, 1927

HOOT HOOT
I SCREAM
1201

California Crazy

HOOT HOOT I SCREAM

Location: 8711 Long Beach Boulevard, South Gate
Date: 1930

MOTHER GOOSE PANTRY

Location: 1929 East Colorado Boulevard, Pasadena
Date: 1929

CABAZON MONSTER

Owner: Claude Bell
Architect: Claude Bell
Location: Interstate 10, Cabazon
Started 1965; completed 1975

California Crazy

THE PUP CAFE

Location: 12732 West Washington Boulevard, Los Angeles
Circa 1930

THE PIG CAFE

Location: Unknown
Date: 1934

California Crazy

THE LEMON

Location: Unknown
Circa 1926

THE PUMPKIN PALACE

Location: 3611 Magnolia Boulevard, Burbank
Date: 1927

LA CAÑA RESTAURANT

Location: Vineland Avenue at Lankershim Boulevard, North Hollywood
Circa 1935

California Crazy

TWIN BARRELS DRIVE-IN

Owner: Joseph Niquette
Location: 1000 East Slauson Avenue, Los Angeles
Date: 1928

KONE INN

Location: 402 York Boulevard, Eagle Rock
Circa 1931

THE BUCKET

Original Location: 4541 Eagle Rock Boulevard, Eagle Rock
Circa 1935

California Crazy

The FREEZER

402

California Crazy

THE FREEZER

Owner: United Sweet Shops
Original Location: 751 South Alvarado, Los Angeles
Date: 1928

SANTA CLAUS, CALIFORNIA

Owners: Ruth and Hap Schaergus
Designer: Pat McKeon
Location: Highway 101, Carpenteria
Date: 1954

THE MUSHROOMS

Location: 3500 South Olive Avenue, Burbank
Date: 1928

THE UMBRELLA SERVICE STATION

Owner: General Petroleum Gas
Location: 830 South LaBrea Avenue, Los Angeles
Date: 1930

California Crazy

BARKIES

Location: 3649 Beverly Boulevard, Los Angeles
Date: 1930

THE DOG HOUSE

Original Location: 1270 North Vermont, Los Angeles
Date: 1963

THE SHOWBOAT

Location: 3242 Cahuenga Boulevard West, Studio City
Date: 1968

THE HOLLYWOOD FLOWER POT

Location: Unknown
Circa 1930

TAUBE PLUMBING

Location: Los Angeles
Circa 1927

THE COCA COLA BOTTLING COMPANY

Architect: Robert V. Derrah
Location: 1334 South Central, Los Angeles
Date: 1936-1937

UNITED EQUIPMENT COMPANY

Owner: Harold Logsdon
Architect: Cliff Cheney
Location: 600 West Glenwood, Turlock
Date: 1977

California Crazy

THE ROUND HOUSE

Location: 250 North Virgil Avenue, Los Angeles
Date: 1927

THE TOONERVILLE TROLLEY

Location: Unknown
Circa 1929

THE JAIL CAFE

Location: 4312 Hollywood Boulevard, Hollywood

THE DUGOUT

Location: 6157 Whittier Boulevard, Montebello
Date: 1927

THE SHELL OIL BUILDING

Location: California Exposition, Balboa Park, San Diego
Date: 1935

ALICE FAYE'S CLUB CAR

Location: Wilshire Boulevard and San Vincente, Los Angeles
Date: 1938

THE BIG FIREPLACE

Location: 5837 Washington Boulevard, Los Angeles
Circa 1930

COBB'S CHICKEN HOUSE

Location: Treasure Island, San Francisco
1939 World's Fair

California Crazy

THE BIG CONE

Owner: C.L. Carter
Location: 1934 South San Fernando Road, Glendale

MAGNUS ROOT BEER

Location: San Francisco, California
Circa 1934

THE ORANGE INN

Location: 2932 Foothill Boulevard, Pasadena
Date: 1923

THE HOT DOG STAND

Location: Oakland, California
Circa 1930

SAMSON TIRE WORKS

Architect: Morgan, Wells and Clemens
Location: 5675 Telegraph Road, City of Commerce
Date: 1929

CHAPTER TWO: PERIOD REVIVAL

THE AZTEC HOTEL

Architect: Robert Stacy-Judd
Location: 311 West Foothill, Monrovia
Date: 1925

California Crazy

THE MAYAN THEATER

Architect: Morgan, Wells and Clemens
Location: 1040 South Hill, Los Angeles
Date: 1927

CALMOS #1 SERVICE STATION

Location: 4982 Hollywood Boulevard, Hollywood
Date: 1925

California Crazy

GIRARD INN

Location: Topanga and Ventura Boulevards, Woodland Hills
Date: 1928

CLIFTON'S SOUTH SEAS CAFETERIA

Owner: Clifford Clinton
Architect: Welton Becket Associates
Location: 618 South Olive, Los Angeles
Date: 1931

California Crazy

THE GRASS SHACK DRIVE-IN

Location: 1911 East Pacific Coast Highway, Long Beach
Circa 1948

GAY'S LION FARM

Location: Valley Boulevard, El Monte
Date: 1926

California Crazy

THE BLACK TENT

Location: South Palm Canyon Drive, Palm Springs
Date: 1937

GRAUMAN'S CHINESE THEATER

Owner: Sid Grauman
Architect: Meyer and Holland
Location: 6925 Hollywood Boulevard, Hollywood
Date: 1927

MANDARIN MARKET

Location: 1248 Vine Street, Hollywood
Date: 1929

California Crazy

THE SPHINX REALTY

Location: 537 North Fairfax, Los Angeles
Date: 1926

California Crazy

THE EGYPTIAN THEATER

Owner: Sid Grauman
Architect: Meyer and Holler
Location: 6712 Hollywood Boulevard, Hollywood
Date: 1922

WILLAT STUDIOS

Owner: Irvin C. Willat
Architect: Henry Oliver
Location: 6509 West Washington Boulevard, Culver City
Date: 1921

California Crazy

TAM O' SHANTER

Owners: Ralph and Harry Van De Kamp
Architect: Henry Oliver
Location: 2930 Los Feliz Boulevard, Glendale
Date: 1922

VAN DE KAMP'S BAKERIES

Owners: Theo. J. Van De Kamp and Lawrence Frank
Architect: Henry Oliver
Location: Store Number One, 248 North Western Avenue, Los Angeles
Date: 1921

TONY'S BURGERS

Owner: Kenneth Bemis
Original Location: 1061 South Hill, Los Angeles
Date: 1930

California Crazy

THE OLD LOG CABIN

Location: University Avenue, San Diego
Date: 1931

MISSION VILLAGE

Location: 5600 West Washington Boulevard, Culver City
Date: 1932

California Crazy

KENYON'S DESERT PLUNGE

Location: El Centro, California
Date: 1929

CAPITOL INN

Location: Junction of U.S. Routes 40 and 99, Sacramento
Date: 1948

THE PLANTATION CAFE

Owner: Roscoe "Fatty" Arbuckle
Contractor: Don Coombs
Location: 7600 West Washington Boulevard, Culver City
1926

SAN DIEGO EGYPTIAN THEATRE

Location: San Diego
Circa 1930

WIGWAM VILLAGE

Location: 2728 Foothill Boulevard, Rialto
Date: 1955

THE CLIFF DWELLERS CAFE

Location: 3585 Beverly Boulevard, Los Angeles
Date: 1927

TOWER AUTO COURT

Location: 10980 Ventura Boulevard, North Hollywood
Date: 1929

California Crazy

R.K.O. STUDIOS

Location: Melrose Avenue and Gower Street
Date: 1934

KINGS TROPICAL INN

Location: 5741 West Washington Boulevard, Culver City
Date: 1926

THE BEVERLY THEATER

Location: 206 North Beverly Drive, Beverly Hills
Date: 1930-31

KMTR RADIO STATION

Location: 1522 North La Brea, Hollywood
Date: 1939

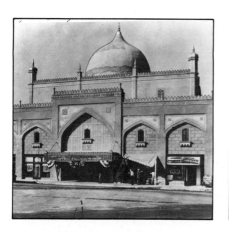

SANDWICHES

TOASTED FRANKFURTS

FRANKFURTS | DINNERS | HAMBURGERS

TOASTED HAMBURGS

Ice Cream

Ice Cream

CHAPTER THREE: OUT-OF-STATE ODDITIES

THE ICE CREAM CARTON

Location: Berlin, Connecticut
Date: October 1939

THE MELON PATCH

Location: Portland, Oregon
Circa 1939

California Crazy

Location: New Bedford, Pennsylvania
Circa 1943

THE PIG

Location: Harlingen, Texas
Circa 1939

California Crazy

THE DOG

Location: U.S. 99, near Lane, Oregon
Circa 1939

THE DERRICK

Location: Oklahoma City, Oklahoma
Circa 1939

California Crazy

THE WIG WAM

Location: Coulee City, Washington
Circa 1939

Location: Laceyville, Pennsylvania
Circa 1946

California Crazy

THE ICE CREAM FREEZER

Location: West Virginia
Date: 1927

A giant Derby, Orange, Shoe, Iceberg, Teepee, Keg, Chili Bowl, Camera, Milk Bottle, Locomotive, Tamale, Fruit Basket, Mountain, Dog, and Hot Dog. They were really the first. Oh, sure, I remember buying donuts on Sundays at a building with a twenty-foot "glazed" perched on top, and I remember my father *never* stopping at those giant oranges on Highway 99, but it wasn't until a 1969 article in the *L.A. Times* Sunday supplement "West" that I really got my first look at the crazy buildings out there somewhere in 450 square miles of urban L.A. From that day on, whenever I ran across a photo, or best of all actually came in contact with one, I jotted down the info, shot a slide, or took a xerox of what soon became a file full of airplane gas stations, immense instamatic cameras, pig-shaped drive-ins, and giant owl ice cream stands.

What became apparent was that this interesting menagerie of architectural aberrations wasn't well documented at all. More obscure photos surfaced, but next to nothing was written about them—a paragraph here, a caption there, but nothing that gave locations, dates or owners. Just pictures.

I began researching in earnest a book about Hollywood nightlife at its zenith —an idea inspired by my parents' during the '30s and '40s at Casa Manana, Zamboanga and the Palladium. A couple of months at the Central Library in downtown L.A. unearthed more photos of oddball buildings and I figured these suckers had me. Five years later I had added three thousand miles

to my car, increased my slide library by several thousand, become a swap-meet and postcard club junkie, and been introduced to a vast network of roadside maniacs. It also honed my research techniques to the point that I was able to identify and date almost all the structures in my files. By checking city directories, the Directory Library of Pacific Telephone Company, back issues of extinct magazines, visiting libraries from Washington D.C. to San Bernardino, unearthing the whereabouts of "lost photographers," and studying (with the assistance of Roleen Heimann and Freda Wheatley-Vizcarra) fifteen years of the weekly *Patent Gazette*, I managed to accumulate an abundance of anecdotes. A sampling:

The owner of the giant tractor in Turlock, California was inspired to erect his structure after visiting Japan where a similar company there had a large tractor perched atop its building. Why not a whole building shaped like one? Click. American ingenuity at its prime.

The origin of Santa Claus, California came from the fact that the particular location of the owner's first stand was situated amidst cities and towns that had the name Santa attached to them, such as Santa Barbara, Santa Maria, and Santa Paula. Thus, Santa Claus, California. Makes sense, doesn't it?

The Brown Derby's origins are legendary. Owner Herbert Somborn, in the course of casual conversation, remarked to a gathering of acquaintances that after considering the sad state of restaurants in L.A. he felt that if you served good-quality, home-cooked meals without all the frills, people would come flocking no matter what you called it. He called it The Brown Derby, constructed his restaurant to look like one, so people wouldn't forget it, and an institution was born overnight.

To insure the illusion of its fairy-tale setting, the Mother Goose Pantry employed waitresses with a maximum height of five feet two inches and a weight of not more than 112 pounds, dressed them in orange, black and white uniforms (the color scheme also used for the exterior of the structure), and covered the interior walls with "folklore paintings." An additional advertising plus resulted whenever improvements were undertaken on the building. Thus, an interior linoleum job became "the installation of the largest insole in the world" and an exterior painting availed the painter to proclaim the adage of "polishing and giving a shine to the largest shoe known to man."

Again in the realm of advertising, The Freezers ice cream chain learned that when their stationary handles were equipped with motors and began to revolve their business doubled the first week. An additional increase in ice cream action occurred when the natural brown colors of the moveable steel structures were transformed to an eye-catching white with red hoops. Sweet success!

Although usually construed in the press as lining the streets, the fact is that most of the structures were spread over a large geographical area. One exception was the intersection of Beverly Blvd., Virgil St. and Temple St. Within a ten-year span, several blocks were blessed with the following: Barkies, the Cliff Dwellers Cafe, a Chili Bowl, The Freezer, a Van de Kamp's windmill and The Roundhouse. Hooray!

The majority of the buildings employed nameless contractors in their construction. Many were designed—some on scraps of paper—by their owners, as in the case of the Shutter Shack, Arthur Whizin's Chili Bowls, and Deschwanden's Shoe Repair. Others could afford bonafide architects for their major commissions and at least three establishments (the Tam O' Shanter, Van de Kamp's and Willat Studios) used Hollywood set designer Henry Oliverto to produce their creations.

The frosting on the proverbial cake came about with the meeting of Arthur Whizin, the sole survivor of Programatic proprietors (or as he calls himself, "The Lone Ranger"). His interview provided a bookload of stories. For instance, the inspiration for his chain came while delivering pies to the proprietor of a restaurant in Santa Ana, California. Tossing him a cracked chili bowl he was going to discard, the owner said, "Do something with it, Whizin." Arthur did. He copied it the following week and nine years later he had eighteen Chili Bowls going, selling to 1,642,000 customers annually. Despite locating the Bowls on strategic

122

corners as the chain grew, the "Chili Bowl King" opened his first unit several blocks from his residence "because I sold my car to open the first restaurant and had to walk to work." The interiors were lit by cloverleaf patterns of red neon and the bathrooms were fitted with blue lights, a fact soon to become a running joke with Jack Benny and Fred Allen on their radio show. Whizin employed a speedboat, an airplane, and sponsored a baseball team to advertise his restaurants. Raffle tickets were given away and the weekly winner was whisked above L.A. or sped to Avalon and back on the Miss Chili Bowl II. A special culinary feature was the endless supply of French rolls and butter to soak up the chili. Whizin claims that any of his staff of collegians could flip a pat of butter to each of the twenty-six stools of his counter from the center of the grill. The stuff nostalgia is made of.

Realizing that the heyday of the Programatic is past us, it is interesting to speculate what a resurgence of these creatures would hold. If the fantasy I've harbored while passing, reading about, and scanning photos of these vernacular beauties would come to pass "in the not too distant future," wouldn't it be great to jump once again into the car to go sampling chili in a giant bowl, or purchase flowers from an oversized pot, or how about pulling up to a stucco pig for a ham on rye, or. . .?

Jim Heimann

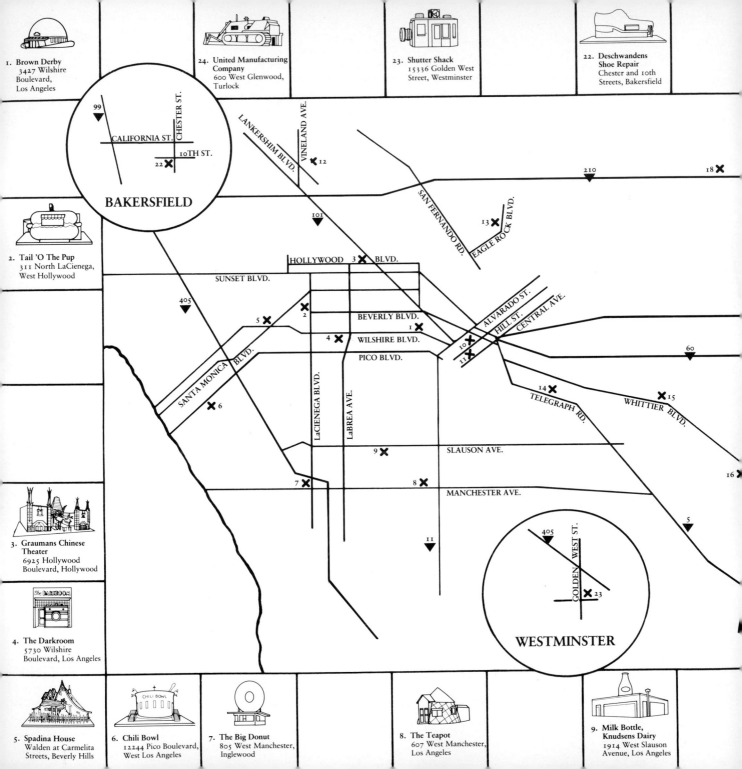

1. **Brown Derby**
3427 Wilshire
Boulevard,
Los Angeles

24. **United Manufacturing
Company**
600 West Glenwood,
Turlock

23. **Shutter Shack**
15336 Golden West
Street, Westminster

22. **Deschwandens
Shoe Repair**
Chester and 10th
Streets, Bakersfield

99

CHESTER ST.
CALIFORNIA ST.
10TH ST.
22

BAKERSFIELD

LANKERSHIM BLVD.
VINELAND AVE.
12

SAN FERNANDO RD.
EAGLE ROCK BLVD.
210
18
13

2. **Tail 'O The Pup**
311 North LaCienega,
West Hollywood

101

HOLLYWOOD 3 BLVD.
SUNSET BLVD.

405
5
2
BEVERLY BLVD.
1
4
WILSHIRE BLVD.
PICO BLVD.

ALVARADO ST.
HILL ST.
CENTRAL AVE.
10
11

SANTA MONICA BLVD.
LaCIENEGA BLVD.
LaBREA AVE.

6

60

14
TELEGRAPH RD.
15
WHITTIER BLVD.

9
SLAUSON AVE.

16

7
8
MANCHESTER AVE.

11

5

405
GOLDEN WEST ST.
23

WESTMINSTER

3. **Graumans Chinese
Theater**
6925 Hollywood
Boulevard, Hollywood

4. **The Darkroom**
5730 Wilshire
Boulevard, Los Angeles

5. **Spadina House**
Walden at Carmelita
Streets, Beverly Hills

6. **Chili Bowl**
12244 Pico Boulevard,
West Los Angeles

7. **The Big Donut**
805 West Manchester,
Inglewood

8. **The Teapot**
607 West Manchester,
Los Angeles

9. **Milk Bottle,
Knudsens Dairy**
1914 West Slauson
Avenue, Los Angeles

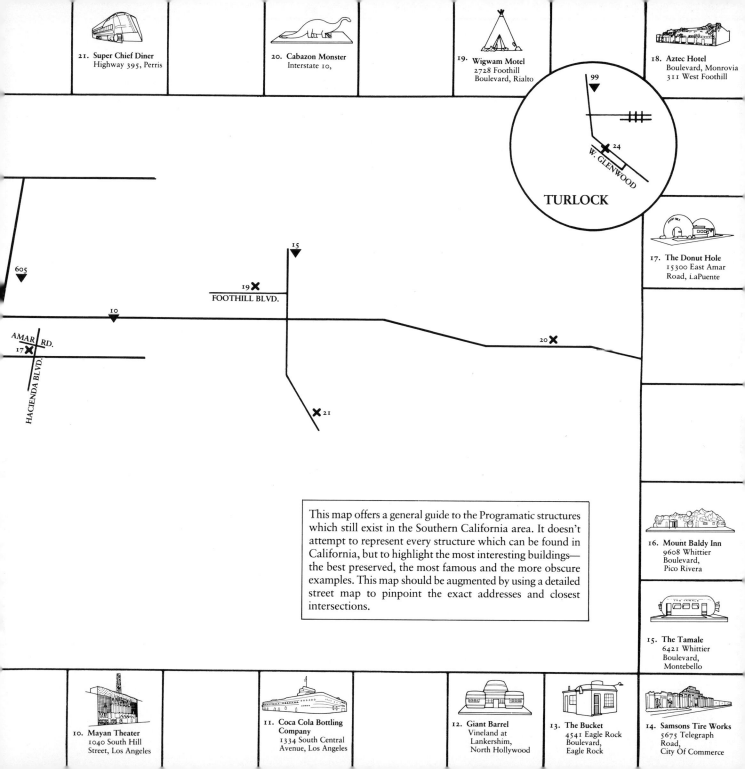

21. **Super Chief Diner**
Highway 395, Perris

20. **Cabazon Monster**
Interstate 10,

19. **Wigwam Motel**
2728 Foothill
Boulevard, Rialto

18. **Aztec Hotel**
Boulevard, Monrovia
311 West Foothill

99

24
W. GLENWOOD

TURLOCK

17. **The Donut Hole**
15300 East Amar
Road, LaPuente

15

605

19 ✗
FOOTHILL BLVD.

10

20 ✗

AMAR RD.
17 ✗

HACIENDA BLVD.

✗ 21

This map offers a general guide to the Programatic structures
which still exist in the Southern California area. It doesn't
attempt to represent every structure which can be found in
California, but to highlight the most interesting buildings—
the best preserved, the most famous and the more obscure
examples. This map should be augmented by using a detailed
street map to pinpoint the exact addresses and closest
intersections.

16. **Mount Baldy Inn**
9608 Whittier
Boulevard,
Pico Rivera

15. **The Tamale**
6421 Whittier
Boulevard,
Montebello

10. **Mayan Theater**
1040 South Hill
Street, Los Angeles

11. **Coca Cola Bottling
Company**
1334 South Central
Avenue, Los Angeles

12. **Giant Barrel**
Vineland at
Lankershim,
North Hollywood

13. **The Bucket**
4541 Eagle Rock
Boulevard,
Eagle Rock

14. **Samsons Tire Works**
5675 Telegraph
Road,
City Of Commerce

1. **John R. Crossland, ed.** *The Modern Marvels Encyclopedia,* (London and Glasgow: Collins Clear-Type Press, 1938), p. 313.

2. "Palaces of The Hot Doges," *Architectural Forum,* vol. 63, August, 1935, pp. 30-31.

3. *The Illustrated Directory of Oakland, California,* (Oakland: The Illustrative Directory Co., 1896), pp. 25-26.

4. **Albert Forbes Sieveking,** *Gardens Ancient and Modern,* (London: Aldine House, 1899), p. 17. The shaping of trees and shrubs into geometric and other forms dates back to early Egyptian period. See Richardson Wright, *The Story of Gardening,* (New York: Dover Publications, 1963), p. 32.

5. In addition to the three French architects, Claude–Nicolas Ledoux, Etienne-Louis Boulée, and Jean Jacques Lequeu, who are the acknowledged masters of the late eighteenth-century Visionary architecture, there were the Germans David and Friedrich Gilly, Karl Friedrich von Schinkel, the Britons Sir John Soane and Joseph Gandy, and the Americans, Benjamin H. Latrobe and Thomas Jefferson. See **Emil Kaufmann,** "Three Revolutionary Architects, Boulée, Ledoux, and Lequeu," *Transactions of the American Philosophical Society,* vol. 42, part 3, (Philadelphia, 1952); *Visionary Architects: Boulée, Ledoux, Lequeu,* (Houston: University of St. Thomas, 1968).

6. **Theodore F. Laist,** "Peculiar Architecture," *American Architect and Building News,* vol. 29, August 9, 1890, pp. 86-89; **Clay Lancaster,** *Architectural Follies in America,* (Rutland, Vermont: Charles E. Tuttle Co., 1960), pp. 186-193; **Julian Cavalier,** "Elephants Remembered," *Historic Preservation,* vol. 29, January-March, 1977, pp. 39-43. An elephant similar to that at Margate City was built by Lafferty at Coney Island.

7. Illustrated in *The Architect and Engineer,* vol. 26, October, 1911, p. 105.

8. "Milk Bottle Architecture," *The Architect and Engineer,* vol. 35, January, 1914, p. 113.

9. **Kenneth M. Murchison,** "As I See It," *The American Architect,* vol. 138, September, 1930, p. 24.

10. *Ibid.,* 1930, p. 25.

11. **Charles Harris Whitaker and Hartley Burr Alexander,** *The Architectural Sculpture of the State Capitol at Lincoln, Nebraska.* (New York: Press of the American Institute of Architects, 1926).

12. **David Gebhard,** *The Richfield Building: 1928-1968,* (New York: The Atlantic

Richfield Co., 1968), p. 16.

13. **Robert H. Orr,** "Sculptural Advertising," *The Architect and Engineer,* vol. 91, October, 1927, p. 27.

14. Illustrated in *Signs of the Times,* vol. 68, June, 1931, p. 31.

15. **H.A. Wood,** "Used Car Marketing," *Signs of the Times,* vol. 66, November, 1930, p. 48; "Milwaukee, Wis.," *Signs of the Times,* vol. 77, August, 1934, pp. 56-57.

16. **H.H. Linsmith,** "One Bulletin Display," *Signs of the Times,* vol. 72, September, 1932, p. 13.

17. **David Gebhard,** "Life in the Dollhouse," *Bay Area Houses,* Sally Woodbridge (Editor), (New York: Oxford University Press, 1976), pp. 99-119. 99-119.

18. "For Streamlined Structures," *Signs of the Times,* vol. 81, December, 1935, pp. 12-14.

19. One of the richer sources for our knowledge of Programatic Architecture is the *Official Gazette* of the U.S. Patent Office; especially the years from 1928 through 1935.

20. The White Tower Chain was established in Milwaukee in 1926. See **Paul Hirshorn** and **Steven Izenour,** *White Tower,* (Cambridge, Massachusetts: M.I.T. Press, 1979).

21. The White Castle system was established in Wichita, Kansas, in 1921. It eventually spread east to New York City. See **E.W. Ingram, Sr.,** *All This From a 5-Cent Hamburger,* (New York: The Newcomen Society in North America, 1970). For examples of White Castle buildings see **David Gebhard and Tom Martinson,** *A Guide to Architecture in Minnesota,* (Minneapolis: University of Minnesota Press, 1977). The Silver Castle system was established in Tulsa, Oklahoma, in 1936, and by 1941 units had been built throughout Oklahoma and parts of Texas.

22. One of the richer sources for our knowledge of Programatic Architecture is the *Official Gazette* of the U.S. Patent Office; especially the years from 1928 through 1935.

23. **J. Edward Tufft,** "The Mother Goose Pantry," *Wayside Salesman,* vol. 1, November, 1931, p. 20.

24. "White Log Taverns," *Pacific Coast Record,* June, 1934, pp. 11 and 12; "Quick Lunch in California," *Fortune,* vol. 16, July, 1937, pp. 90-94.

25. **Sam F. Goddard,** "From Footlights to Fireplace," *Pacific Coast Record,* vol.

18, April, 1927, pp. 21-22.

26. "New Studio is Novelty," *Los Angeles Express*, April 6, 1921, p. 19. This building was later remodeled and moved to Beverly Hills, and became known as the Spadena Residence.

27. *Ibid.*, 1921, p. 19.

28. The first of the Van De Kamp's Bakery buildings with the windmill motif was built in 1921 in Los Angeles at the corner of Western and Beverly Boulevards. The initial name for The Tam O'Shanter Inn was Montgomery's County Inn.

29. "Tam O'Shanter," *Pacific Coast Record*, vol. 29, September, 1938, pp. 14-15.

30. *Ibid.*, 1938, p. 14.

31. "Cross Roads of The World," *California Arts and Architecture*, vol. 51, January, 1937, p. 24.

32. "Aztec Breathes of Olden Days," *Pacific Coast Record*, vol. 16, October, 1925, pp. 1-2; **Joe Minster**, "Soboba Indian Village, *Pacific Coast Record*, vol. 18, July, 1927, pp. 1-3.

33. **Morrow Mayo,** *Los Angeles* (New York: Alfred A. Knopf, 1933); The two pages of photos of Programatic buildings bear the caption: "Some of The Bizarre Restaurants and Refreshment Stands which delight the eye and tickle the Palate of visitors to Los Angeles." See also "Weird Architecture Helps to Sell Ice Cream," *Popular Mechanics*, vol. 49, January, 1928, p. 101; "Wayside Inns Around Los Angeles," *Wayside Salesman*, vol. 1, November 1930, pp. 20-21; "Many Unique Refreshment Stands Adorn Southern California Highways," *Wayside Salesman*, vol. 1, July, 1930, pp. 16-17. "Palaces of The Hot Doges," *Architectural Forum*, vol. 63, August, 1935, pp. 30-31.

34. **Annette Del Zeppo and Jeffrey Stanton,** *Venice, California, 1904-1930*, (Venice, Calif.: ARS Publications, 1978).

35. "The Coca Cola Plant, Los Angeles, California," *California Arts and Architecture*, vol. 50, November, 1936, p. 43.

36. "All Aboard the Sky Liner," *Pacific Coast Record*, vol. 29, July, 1938, p. 16.

37. "California Boom," *Life*, vol. 20, June 10, 1946, p. 31.

38. The form of the doughnut for a Programatic building dates from the 1939 New York World's Fair, where the respected firm of Skidmore and Owings designed with John Moss a Wonder Bakers building using this theme. See *Architect and Engineer*, vol. 137, January, 1938, p. 8.

39. Illusionary signage which played off real buildings against perspective murals suggesting buildings and landscape were illustrated from time to time in the pages of *Signs of the Time*. For example see the illustration of Vernor's Ginger Ale Building and sign in Flint, Michigan, *Signs of the Time*, vol. 74, August, 1933, p. 24.

40. **Robert H. Orr,** "Sculptural Advertising," *The Architect and Engineer*, vol. 91, October, 1927, p. 54.

41. **Henry Russell Hitchcock,** *The Architecture of H.H. Richardson and His Times,* (New York: Museum of Modern Art, 1936), pp. 302-303.

42. "Tourism and Mobility," *Landscape*, vol. 9, no. 3, Spring, 1962, pp. 1-27; "The Evolving Strip," *Landscape*, vol. 16, no. 3, Spring, 1967, p. 2.

43. **Robert Venturi,** *Complexity and Contradiction in Architecture*, (New York: Museum of Modern Art, 1965); and **Robert Venturi, Denise Scott Brown and Steven Izenour,** *Learning from Las Vegas*, (Cambridge, Massachusetts: M.I.T. Press, 1972). Another early exponent of programatic architecture is the Viennese architect Hans Hollein, who in the early 1960s asked why we might not use the form of an aircraft carrier for a city, or the form of a spark plug or a Rolls Royce radiator grill for a high-rise building. See *Hollein*, catalogue published for the exhibition, (Chicago: Richard Feigen Gallery, 1969). There have been several recent publications which have explored programatic aspects of the commercial vernacular. These include **Marc Treib,** "Eye-Konism, Part 1," *Print*, Vol. 27, March/April, 1973, pp. 68-73; "Eye-Konism, Part 2," *Print*, Vol, 27, May/June, 1973, pp. 54-60, 104; **John Baeder,** *Diners*, (New York: Abrams, 1978); **Paul Hirshorn and Steven Izenour,** *White Tower*, (Cambridge, Massachusetts: M.I.T. Press, 1979); **Daniel I. Vieyra,** *Fill 'er Up: An Architectural History of America's Gas Stations*, (New York: Collier Books, 1979); **Richard J.S. Gutman and Elliott Kaufman,** *American Diner*, (New York: Harper and Row, 1979).

44. The Maurer Duck at Riverhead was illustrated and discussed in "Duck-Shaped Building Advertises Roadside Business," *Roadside Merchant*, vol. 5, May, 1934, p. 7.

BIBLIOGRAPHY

Anon. *The Architect and Engineer.* Vol. 26. October, 1911. p. 105.

——. "New Studio Is Novelty, Style Two Centuries Old Copied." *Los Angeles Express.* Vol. 51, no. 9. April 6, 1921. p. 19.

——. "Polishing Largest Size Milk Bottle." *Los Angeles Times.* August 10, 1927. Part V, p. 9.

——. "Weird Architecture Helps Sell Ice Cream." *Popular Mechanics.* Vol. 49. January, 1928. p. 101.

——. "How 'Glorified' Ice Cream Stands Advertise and Sell the Product." *The Ice Cream Trade Journal.* Vol. 24. March, 1928. pp. 46-48.

——. "Ice Cream Stand Like Igloo Helps Draw Crowds." *Popular Mechanics.* Vol. 49. July, 1928. p. 47.

——. "Mr. Jenkins and Mr. Henri, Shell Oil in the U.S." *Fortune.* Vol. 6. October, 1932. pp. 32-37.

——. "Wonders of the Chicago World's Fair." *Modern Mechanix and Iventions.* Vol. 10. September, 1933. p. 67.

——. "The Great American Roadside." *Fortune.* Vol. 10. September, 1934. pp. 53-63.

——. "Shell Oil Company Building." *Architect and Engineer.* Vol. 121. June, 1935. pp. 15-18.

——. "Palaces of the Hot Doges." *Architectural Forum.* Vol. 63. August, 1935. pp. 30-31.

——. *Arrowhead Magazine.* November, 1935. pp. 13-15.

——. *Pictorial California.* Vol. 10. 1936. p. 9.

——. "Cross Roads of the World." *California Arts and Architecture.* Vol. 51. January, 1937. pp. 24-25.

——. *Westways.* Vol. 29. April, 1937. p. 10.

——. "California Boom." *Life.* Vol. 20. June, 10, 1946. p. 31.

——. "World-Famed Ship Cafe On Auction Block Today." *Los Angeles Times.* Vol. 65, part I. October 17, 1946. p. 1.

——. "California Sunstruck Signs." *Holiday.* Vol. 11. January, 1947. pp. 45-46.

_____. "The Streamlining of Outdoor Advertising Structures," *Signs of the Times,* Vol. 89, October, 1947, pp. 54, 56, 58, 59.

_____. "Low Camp." *Los Angeles Federal Savings Magazine.* Winter, 1966.

_____. "Dreamers and Doers." *U.C.L.A. Librarian.* Vol. 27. March, 1974. pp. 13-14.

_____. "Only in Southern California: Claude Bell Builds Himself a Brontosaurus." *People Weekly.* Vol. 3. June 23, 1975. pp. 66-67.

_____. *Historic Preservation Element.* City of Glendale, California Planning Division. 1977. pp. 51-56.

Ant Farm. *Automerica.* New York: Dutton Books, 1976.

Baeder, John. *Diners.* New York: Abrams, 1978.

Banham, Reyner. *Los Angeles: The Architecture of Four Ecologies.* London: Harper & Row, 1974.

Brown, Curtis F. *Star Spangled Kitsch.* New York: Universe Books, 1975.

Carroll, Jerry. "Where Did The Giant Orange Go?" *San Francisco Chronicle.* July 29, 1973.

Chamberlain, J.L. "Denver Gets Something Different," *Signs of the Times,* Vol. 89, May, 1937, pp. 22, 111. (Yacht Club Restaurant in form of a ship, designed by John Hicks).

Crossland, John. *The Modern Marvels Encyclopedia.* London and Glasgow: Collins Clear-Type Press, 1938. pp. 313-318.

Dietz, Lawrence. "There Was Once A Woman Who Lived In A Shoe." *West Magazine of the Los Angeles Times.* November 30, 1969. pp. 12-15.

Faris, Gerald. "Facade of Fantasy Is Up For Sale." *Los Angeles Times.* Part 1. August 29, 1979. p. 3.

Fishwick, Marshall and Neil J. Meredith. *Popular Architecture.* Bowling Green: Popular Press, 1975.

Gebhard, David and Tom Martinson. *A Guide to Architecture in Minnesota.* Minneapolis: University of Minnesota Press, 1977.

Gebhard, David, Roger Montgomery, Robert Winter, John Woodbridge, and Sally Woodbridge. *A Guide to Architecture in San Francisco and Northern California.* Santa Barbara: Peregrine Smith, 1973.

Gebhard, David and Harriette Von Breton, *1868-1967: Architecture in California.* Santa Barbara, UCSB Art Museum, 1968.

Gebhard, David and Harriette Von Breton. *L.A. in the Thirties.* Salt Lake City: Peregrine Smith, 1975.

Gebhard, David and Robert Winter. *A Guide to Architecture in Los Angeles and Southern California.* Salt Lake City: Peregrine Smith, 1977.

Gutman, Richard and Elliott Kaufman. *American Diner.* New York: Harper & Row, 1979.

Hancock, Ralph. "The Brown Derby." *Fabulous Boulevard.* New York: Funk & Wagnalls, 1949. pp. 299-301.

Hill, Douglas. *Camera.* Vol. 5. May, 1978. pp. 24-32.

Hirshorn, Paul and Steven Izenour. *White Towers.* Cambridge, Mass.: M.I.T. Press, 1979.

Ingram, E.W., Sr. *All This From A 5-Cent Hamburger.* New York: The Newcomen Society in North America, 1970.

Jenks, Charles. *Bizarre Architecture.* New York: Rizzoli Books, 1979.

Knight, Carelton. "Roadside Riches." *Preservation News.* Vol. 30. January-March, 1978. p. 7.

Laist, Theo. F. "Peculiar Architecture." *American Architect and Building News.* Vol. 29. August 9, 1890. pp. 86-89.

La Wall, G.R. "Luminous Structures As Beer Merchandisers." *Signs of the Times.* Vol. 74. June, 1933. pp. 20-21.

Liebs, Chester. "Remember Our Not-So-Distant Past?" *Historic Preservation.* Vol. 30. January-March, 1978. pp. 30-35.

Mayo, Morrow. *Los Angeles.* New York: Knopf, 1933. pp. 178-179.

McMichael, Stanley L. and Robert F. Bingham. *City Growth Essentials.* Cleveland: The Stanley McMichael Pub. Organization, 1928.

Moran, Thomas. "L.A. Pop Architecture." *Los Angeles Free Press.* Vol. 13. April 2-8, 1976. pp. 6-7.

Moran, Tom and Tom Sewell. *Fantasy by the Sea.* Venice, California: Beyond Baroque Foundation, 1979.

National Petroleum News

Vol. 19. May 18, 1927. "Indians Perform at Mission Style Station Opening." p. 75.

Vol. 19. May 25, 1927. "Filling Station Mistaken For Memorial." p. 107.

Vol. 20. March 7, 1928. "The Original Beacon Stations." p. 91.

Vol. 20. April 18, 1928. "Super Station Designed As Mosque." p. 93.

Vol. 20. April 18, 1928. "Farmer's Silo Advertises Wadhams Oil." p. 80.

Vol. 20. May 16, 1928. "Prize Winning Roadside Stands." p. 93.

Vol. 20. June 13, 1928. "200 Moroccan Styled Stations Planned For Cuba." p. 84.

Vol. 20. September 12, 1928. "Looks Like Airplane—It's Really A Filling Station." p. 19.

Vol. 20. September 29, 1928. "Portable Country Stations Are Replicas of Famous Lighthouse." p. 68.

Vol. 21. April 24, 1929. "Wooden Indian Gets New Lease On Life As Gasoline Trade Puller." pp. 112-115.

Vol. 21. June 19, 1929. "Seashore Gasoline Station Modeled After Ship." p. 112.

Vol. 22. March 19, 1930. "Chinese Pagoda Motif For Wadhams Service Stations." p. 179.

Vol. 22. April 13, 1930. "Lighthouse Gas Station Opens In Tulsa." p. 38.

Vol. 22. April 30, 1930. "Tourist Camp Stations Patterned After Dutch Windmill." p. 105 & 108.

Vol. 22. June 25, 1930. "Indian Village To Grow Around Station." p. 89.

Vol. 22. November 12, 1930. "Station Modeled After Tank Car." p. 206.

Vol. 23. November 25, 1931. "Airplane Service Station." p. 50.

Vol. 24. March 9, 1932. "Egypt Dictates Style For Station." p. 44.

Oberhand, Robert. *The Chili Bowls of Los Angeles.* Published for Los Angeles Institute of Contemporary Art, Los Angeles, 1977.

Onosko, Tim. "The Roadside Stand Goes High Hat." *Wasn't The Future Wonderful?* New York: Dutton Books, 1979. pp. 122-123.

Orr, Robert. "Sculptural Advertising." *Architect and Engineer.* Vol. 91. October, 1927. pp. 53-55.

Pacific Coast Record

Vol. 16. October, 1925. "Aztec Breathes of Olden Days." pp. 5-9.

Vol. 18. April, 1927. "From Footlights To Fireplace." pp. 21-22.

Vol. 18. July, 1927. "Soboba Indian Village." pp. 5-9.

Vol. 18. July, 1927. "Eating in a Tree." p. 23.

Vol. 25. June, 1934. "White Log Taverns." pp. 11-12.

Vol. 29. July, 1938. "All Aboard the Skyliner." p. 16.

Vol. 29. September, 1938. "Tam O'Shanter." p. 14-15.

Vol. 31. February, 1941. "Streamlined Diner." p. 19.

Pastier, John. "The Last Chord of Los Angeles' Piano Landmark." *Los Angeles Times.* Part 4. July 2, 1973. p. 8.

Pennington, Lucinda and Wm. Baxter. *A Past To Remember. The History of Culver City.* Culver City, 1976. pp. 57-68.

Perry, George Sessions. "The Cities of America—Los Angeles." *Saturday Evening Post.* Vol. 218. December 15, 1945. pp. 14-15.

Pildas, Ave. *Art Deco Los Angeles.* New York: Harper & Row, 1977.

Roadside Merchant, Vol. 5. "Duck-Shaped Building Advertises Roadside Business." May 1934. p. 7.

Rosen, Seymour. *In Celebration of Ourselves.* San Francisco: California Living Books, 1979.

Simpich, Frederick. "Southern California At Work." *National Geographic.* Vol. 66. *November, 1934. pp. 544 and 554.*

Treib, Marc. "Eye-Konism, Part 1." *Print.* Vol. 27. March/April, 1973. pp. 68-72.

_____. "Eye-Konism, Part 2: Signs as Buildings as Signs." *Print.* Vol. 27. May/June, 1973. pp. 54-60.

_____. "Alphabets Buildings Cities." *Print.* Vol. 32. May/June, 1978. pp. 47-53.

Tufft, J. Edward. "Chain Stores As Profitable Outlets For California Manufacturers." *The Ice Cream Trade Journal.* Vol. 25. November, 1929. pp. 43-46.

Venturi, Robert, Denise Scott Brown, Steven Izenour. *Learning From Las Vegas.* Cambridge: M.I.T. Press, 1972.

Vieyra, Daniel. *Fill 'er Up.* New York: Collier Books, 1979.

The Wayside Salesman

"Something New In Roadside Stands." June, 1930. pp. 24-25.

"Southern California Highways." July, 1930. pp. 16-17.

"The Orange Inn." July, 1930. pp. 22-23.

"Chapman's Ice Cream" (cover). August, 1930. p. 20.

"The Fenton Sandwich Shop." October, 1930. pp. 7-9.

"Wayside Inns Around Los Angeles." November, 1930. pp. 20-21.

"Tee-Pee Barbeque" (cover). June, 1931.

"The 19th Hole Refreshment Stand." October, 1931. p. 21.

"The Mother Goose Pantry," by Edward Tufft. November, 1931. pp. 20-21.

"The Big Chief." December, 1931. p. 15.

"The Teapot" (cover). February, 1932.

"A Barrel-Full of Profit," by Edgar M. Curtis. March, 1932. p. 7.

Yavno, Max and Lee Shippey. *The Los Angeles Book*. Cambridge, Massachusetts: Houghton Mifflin, 1950. pp. 98-99.

Airplane Cafe 38
Arbuckle, Fatty 21, 107
Aztec Hotel 22, 84

Barkies 24, 72
Beverly Theater 22, 109
Bob's Air Mail Service 26, 27
The Big Cone 81
The Big Donut 23
The Big Fireplace 20, 80
The Black Tent 93
Boulee, Etienne Louis 14
Brown Derby 24, 37, 121, 122
Bryant, Leland A. 16

Cabazon Monster 58-59
Calmos #1 Service 21, 86
Calpet Service Station 21, 88-89
Capitol Inn 106
Chili Bowl 34, 122, 123
The Cliff Dwellers Cafe 21, 108
Clifton's South Seas Cafeteria 24, 90
The Club Car 23, 80
Coate, Roland E. 21
Cobb's Chicken House 23, 80
Coca Cola Bottling Company 21, 77
The Coffee Pot 113

The Darkroom 23, 48
Robert V. Derrah 21, 23
The Derrick 116
Deschwanden's Shoe Repair 40
Dog Cafe 51
Dog House 73
Dog Stand 115
The Donut Hole 23, 53
The Dugout 79

Egyptian Theater, Hollywood 11, 20
22, 97

Egyptian Theater, San Diego 108
Egyptian Village 22

Farmer John's Meat Packing Plant 24
Farver, Rick and Associates 21
Faye's, Alice 23, 80
The Freezer 68

Gay's Lion Farm 92
Girard Inn 22, 87
Goodhue, Bertram G. 16
Grass Shack 91
Grauman's Chinese Theater 11, 20,
22, 94

Hitchcock, Henry Russell 25
Hollywood Flower Pot 75
Hoot Hoot I Scream 22, 23, 56
Hot Cha 31
The Hot Dog 81

Ice Cream Carton 110-111
Ice Cream Freezer 119
Ice Palace 47
Igloo 23, 46

Jackson, J. Brickerhoff 25
The Jail House 79
Judd, Robert-Stacy 22

Kenney, Albert 23
Kenyon's Desert Plunge 105
King's Tropical Inn 22, 109
The Knockout 44

La Cana 64
Lafferty, James F. 15
Ledoux, Claude-Nicolas 14, 15
LeMaire, Charlie 23
The Lemon 62

Lequeu, Jaques 15
Little Mary's Lighthouse Realty 29

Magnus Root Beer Stand 81
Mandarin Market 22, 95
Manning's Big Red Piano 33
Mayan Theater 11, 20, 22, 85
Melon Patch 112
Meyer and Holler 11
Mission Village 104
Morgan, Wells, and Clements 12, 16
Mother Goose Pantry 20, 23, 57
Mount Baldy Inn 55
The Mushrooms 70

Noah's Ark 54

Oil Patch Liquor 45
Old Log Cabin 20, 103
Oliver, Henry 20
Orange Inn 81
Orr, Robert 17

Pierpont and Walter S. Davis 21
The Pig Cafe 114
The Pig Stand Cafe 61
Plantation Club 21, 107
Pumpkin Palace 63
Pup Cafe 60

Randy's Donut 52
Red Keg Drive-In 42-43
Richfield Building 16
R.K.O. Studios 109
The Round House 79

Samson Tire Works (U.S. Royal Tires)

11, 82-83
Sander's System Ben Hur Coffee Pot 30
Sanderson's Stockings 4, 24, 41
Santa Claus 24, 69
Shell Oil Building 80
The Showboat 74
Shutter Shack 49
Sombrero 28
Sphinx Realty 23, 96

Tamale Restaurant 23, 35
Tam O' Shanter 21, 99
Taube Plumbing 76
Theodores School of Music 32
Toed Inn Cover, 24, 50
Tony's Burgers (White Log Tavern) 102
Toonerville Trolley 79
Tower Auto Court 108
Twin Barrels Cafe 65

Umbrella Service Station 71
United Equipment Company 78

Van Alen, William 16
Van De Kamp's 21, 100-101
Venturi, Robert 25

White Castle 18
White Log Taverns 20, 102
White Tower Hamburger Shops 18
Wigwam Stand 117
Wigwam Village 23, 108
Willat Studios 98
Windmill Service Station 118

Zep Diner 39

American Stock Photo 50, 63, 68, 70
John Baeder Collection 119
California Historical Society 80
Jim Deesing Collection 28
David Gebhard, University Art
  Museum, University of California
  Santa Barbara 32
Richard Gutman Collection 79
Jim Heimann Collection 48, 95, 108
Huntington Library 60
Huntington Library/Whittington
  Collection 82, 87, 92
Gary Krueger 36, 37, 40
Library of Congress, Washington,
  D.C. 62, 110-111 (Photographer
  Unknown), 112 (Thurber), 113
  (Esther Bubley), 114 (Russell Lee),
  115 (Dorthea Lange), 116 (Russell
  Lee), 117 (Dorthea Lange), 118
  (Photographer Unknown)
Richard Litt 58-59
Harold Logsden/United
  Manufacturing Company 78
Los Angeles County Museum of
  Natural History 29
Los Angeles Public Library 104, 109
Merriman Photography 86, 88-89
M.G.M. Studios/Research
  Department 43, 75, 108
Alison Morley 52, 53, 55, 67, 73, 74
  102
National Archives, Washington, D.C.

57, 72, 91, 106, 108
New York Public Library 81
Jane O'Neal 31, 45, 49, 64
Pomona Public Library/Frasher
  Collection 26, 27, 54, 93, 105
Marvin Rand 77
San Diego Historical Society 103, 108
Security Pacific National Bank/
  Historical Collections 46, 61, 107
Tom Sewell/Environmental
  Communications 33
The Stock Market/Burton Holmes
  Collection Cover, 30, 51, 65, 66
University of California, Los Angeles
  Special Collections 56, 90
University of California, Los Angeles
  Department of Geography/Burton
  Holmes Collection 47, 75, 80, 95, 96
University of California, Santa Barbara
  Art Museum 84
University of Southern California,
  Doheny Library 80
Marc Wanamaker/Bison Archives
  97, 98
Warner Brothers Inc. 44
Delmar Watson Photography 35, 38,
  39, 76, 79
Dick Whittington Photography 85,
  99, 100-101, 109
Arthur Whizin 34
Robert Winter Collection 71
Max Yavno Frontispiece, 41

139

This book has been designed by
Rip Georges, Hermosa Beach,
California.

The type is Sabon Antigua, designed
by Jan Teischold in 1967, and is
based on the early fonts engraved by
Granjon and Garamond.

The book has been set by
Laura Gest Winder of Gestype,
San Francisco, California.

Chronicle Books
One Hallidie Plaza
San Francisco, California
94102